How to Sparkle at
Reading
Comprehension

Jonny Zucker

Brilliant
PUBLICATIONS

We hope you and your class enjoy using this book. Other books in the series include:

English titles

How to Sparkle at Alphabet Skills	978 1 897675 17 5
How to Sparkle at Grammar and Punctuation	978 1 897675 19 9
How to Sparkle at Phonics	978 1 897675 14 4
How to Sparkle at Prediction Skills	978 1 897675 15 1
How to Sparkle at Word Level Activities	978 1 897675 90 8
How to Sparkle at Writing Stories and Poems	978 1 897675 18 2
How to Sparkle at Nursery Rhymes	978 1 897675 16 8

Maths titles

How to Sparkle at Counting to 10	978 1 897675 27 4
How to Sparkle at Number Bonds	978 1 897675 34 2
How to Sparkle at Addition and Subtraction to 20	978 1 897675 28 1
How to Sparkle at Beginning Multiplication and Division	978 1 897675 30 4
How to Sparkle at Maths Fun	978 1 897675 86 1

Science titles

How to Sparkle at Assessing Science	978 1 897675 20 5
How to Sparkle at Science Investigations	978 1 897675 36 6

Festive title

How to Sparkle at Christmas Time	978 1 897675 62 5

To find out more details on any of our resources, please log onto our website: www.brilliantpublications.co.uk.

Published by Brilliant Publications
Unit 10, Sparrow Hall Farm, Edlesborough, Dunstable, Bedfordshire, LU6 2ES, UK

General information enquiries:
Tel: 01525 222292
E-mail: brilliant@bebc.co.uk
Website: www.brilliantpublications.co.uk

The name Brilliant Publications and the logo are registered trademarks.

Written by Jonny Zucker
Illustrated by Val Edgar

Printed in the UK. First published in 2003. Reprinted 2006 and 2009.
10 9 8 7 6 5 4 3

© Jonny Zucker 2003
Printed ISBN 978 1 903853 44 3
ebook ISBN 978 0 85747 065 2

Contents

Introduction

This book has been designed to provide you with a whole host of KS1 comprehension activities to use in the twenty minutes of independent work in the literacy hour.

Each activity covers at least one comprehension objective of the National Literacy Strategy. All the activities have been created by a practising KS1 teacher and have all been tried out in class. They should save you hours of preparation and planning time and as each sheet is photocopiable the activities can be used time and time again.

Each activity is fun and should inspire your children to read and understand a whole variety of texts. The activities can be used to follow up shared work that you cover in the first fifteen minutes of the lesson. However, each activity is a 'stand alone' piece of work and so can also be used independently by children to enhance their comprehension skills.

How to use this book

The activities in this book have been organized so that children can progress through them, but you can also pick and choose tasks where they meet your needs, for example lower ability children could work on completing the cartoon strips on pages 36 and 37 whilst more able children could work on the comprehension passages such as *School play* on page 46.

Most activities have a limited amount of text at the top so that children can read this and use it as a basis for completing the activity. However, it is vital to talk through each sheet first to explain and demonstrate how you as a teacher would approach the task.

The sheets can be used as a whole class activity, by a small group or in a one-to-one situation.

Classroom environment

Comprehension skills are needed by children in every situation they face and thus your classroom should reflect and enhance these skills. Word banks and dictionaries should be easily accessible. Word lists referring to specific parts of language should be clearly displayed, for example *Question words, Time words*.

Displays relating to comprehension terms can point children in the right direction. Words such as 'fiction' and 'non-fiction' should be on show next to a range of related texts.

To make the study of characters more fun, a character board can be displayed on to which children can add characters from around the school, detailing their main characteristics. To aid work on captions and instructions, you can display simple labelled diagrams or recipes cut out from magazines.

Above all make the activities exciting and encourage children to use their existing knowledge and classroom resources to crack the comprehension tasks in this book.

Links to the National Literacy Strategy

Underpinning all of the activities in this book are the following NLS text-level comprehension objectives:

1. To reinforce and apply word-level skills through reading
2. To use phonological, contextual, grammatical and graphic knowledge to work out, predict and check the meanings of unfamiliar words and to make sense of what they read
3. To notice the difference between spoken and written forms
4. To read simple stories and poems independently

The following NLS text-level objectives apply to specific activities:

Y1.T1.12	To read and use captions (Classroom labels, page 6)
Y1.T1.13	To read and follow simple instructions (Park jumbled sentences, page 17)
Y1.T2.4	To retell stories, giving the main points in sequence (Retelling a story 1 and 2, pages 10 and 11)
Y1.T2.7	To discuss reasons for, or causes of, incidents in stories (The farm trip, page 42; Playground problems, page 44; School play, page 46)
Y1.T2.8	To identify and discuss characters
Y1.T2.10	To identify and compare the basic story elements of beginnings and endings (Beginnings and endings, page 16)
Y1.T2.17	To use the terms 'fiction' and 'non-fiction'
Y1.T3.7	To use titles and 'blurbs' to predict the content of unfamiliar stories (Titles 1 and 2, pages 20 and 21; Blurbs, page 22)
Y1.T3.9	To read a variety of poems on similar themes
Y1.T3.10	To compare and contrast preferences and common themes in stories and poems (Poems on the same theme, page 24)
Y1.T3.18	To use words like *first, next, after, when* (First, next, after, when, page 12)
Y1.T3.19	To identify simple questions (Question marks and exclamation marks, page 33)
Y2.T1.4	To understand time and sequential relationships in stories (Before, during, at the end of, after, page 13; Cartoon strip 1 and 2, pages 36 and 37)
Y2.T1.13	To read simple written instructions in the classroom (Recipe jumble, page 7; Rollerblade instructions, page 8; Class lesson chart, page 9)
Y2.T2.6	To identify and describe characters (Characters 1 and 2, pages 14 and 15)
Y2.T2.9	To identify and discuss patterns of rhyme (Rhyme time, page 25)
Y2.T2.16	To use dictionaries and glossaries to locate words by using initial letter (Dictionaries 1 and 2, pages 28 and 29)
Y2.T2.18	To use alphabetically ordered texts, e.g. registers (Favourite food alphabet list, page 30; Class register, page 31)
Y2.T3.8	To discuss meanings of words and phrases that create humour, and sound effects in poetry, e.g. nonsense poems (What a load of rubbish, page 32)
Y2.T3.13	To understand the distinction between fact and fiction (Fact or fiction? 1 and 2, pages 18 and 19)
Y2.T3.14	To pose questions and record these in writing (Questions 1 and 2, pages 26 and 27)
Y2.T3.16	To scan a text to find specific sections, for example key words or phrases (Key words 1 and 2, pages 34 and 35)

Classroom labels

Draw a line from each word to the object that it names in the classroom.

Computer	Bookcase	Window

Desk	Sink	Chair	Pencil

Poster	Television	Painting

Write out labels for three more objects in the classroom. Draw an arrow from the labels to these objects.

Colour the star if you can spot the toy car.

Recipe jumble

Unscramble these recipe instructions to make a delicious chocolate cake. Write out the correct instructions underneath each one.

2 Crack into bowl eggs a mixing

_____

self-raising in 3 spoons flour Pour of

_____

spoons Add sugar 2 of

_____

spoons 3 powder Put in of chocolate

_____

milk tablespoon in Pour a of

_____

together all of ingredients Mix these

_____

cake Pour mixture tin the baking into a

_____

_____

Ask an adult to help you put the cake in a hot oven for half an hour.

Rollerblade instructions

Here are some instructions for going rollerblading. Write them in the correct order.

Tie up the laces.

Start rollerblading.

Find the rollerblades.

Stand up in the rollerblades.

Put on the thick socks.

Pull on the rollerblades.

Fetch a pair of thick socks.

1._____

2._____

3._____

4._____

5._____

6._____

7._____

Class lesson chart

This is a chart showing what Class 2B do each morning of the week. Look at it carefully and answer the questions below.

Day	1st Lesson	2nd Lesson	3rd Lesson
Monday	Maths	Music	English
Tuesday	English	Science	PE
Wednesday	History	Maths	English
Thursday	English	Dance	Geography
Friday	English	Games	Assembly

1. What do the class do in the third lesson on Monday?

   _____

2. What do they do in the first lesson on Tuesday?

   _____

3. What do they do in the third lesson on Wednesday?

   _____

4. When do they do Dance?

   _____

5. When do they have their Games lesson?

   _____

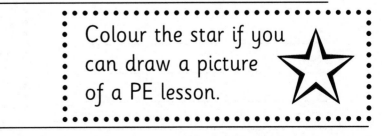

Colour the star if you can draw a picture of a PE lesson.

Retelling a story 1

Read this passage about Sally's Monday morning.

It was Monday morning and Sally woke up twenty minutes late for school. She quickly ate a piece of toast but spilt her orange juice on the kitchen floor. On the way to school she fell over and grazed her knee. Then she ran into class and knocked over the paint pots. It really hadn't been Sally's morning!

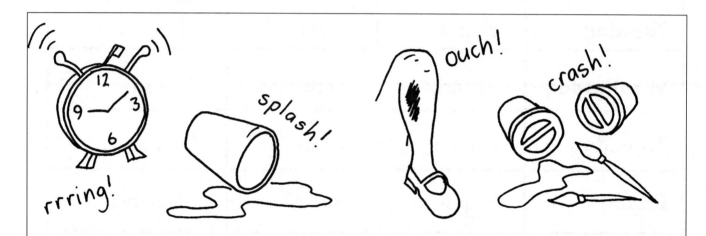

Now imagine that you are Sally. Write about your Monday morning and describe some of the things that go wrong for you.

_____

_____

_____

_____

Think of two other things that might have gone wrong for Sally on that Monday morning.

_____

_____

_____

_____

Colour the star if you can read these to a friend. ★

Retelling a story 2

Read this short story. When you've finished make a list of the main points from the story in the order that they happen.

Sanjay and Lisa were skateboarding in the park. Some big children came over to them and asked for a go on their skateboards. Sanjay said no, and he sped away on his skateboard with Lisa close behind him. The big children ran after them, but Sanjay and Lisa hid behind a bush. They were afraid that the big children would find them.

They didn't need to worry. The park keeper walked straight over to the big children and said to them, "Leave those smaller children alone."

The big children ran off and Sanjay and Lisa enjoyed the rest of the afternoon.

Main points from the story

1. _____

2. _____

3. _____

4. _____

_____

5. _____

_____

First, next, after, when

Read the passage below about a trip to the swimming pool.

First Mum drove us to the local pool in her car. **Next** we got changed into our swimming costumes. **After** changing, we jumped into the pool and swam for over an hour. **When** we had finished swimming, Mum drove us home.

Now write a passage of four sentences about going to a friend's birthday party. Be sure to use the words **first**, **next**, **after**, **when**.

_____

_____

_____

_____

Write and draw two things that you do before you go to bed.

1. _____

2. _____

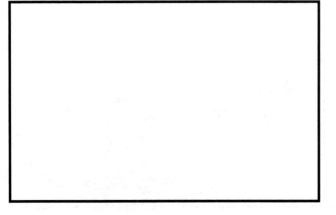

Before, during, at the end of, after

The Match is a poem that looks at the different times of a football match: **before**, **during**, **at the end of** and **after**.

The Match

Before

The football match
I put on my boots
Pull on my shirt
Run to the park.

During

The football match
I pass to the others
Control the ball
Score loads of goals.

At the end of

The football match
I shake hands with everyone
Trot to the changing rooms
Wave to the pretend crowd.

After

The football match
I have a hot shower
Drink a glass of milk
Dream about playing for my favourite team.

Now write a poem called The School Day. Make a list of all the things you do before, during, at the end of and after your day in school. Choose the most interesting ones, and then shape them into a poem like the one above, with four verses.

Colour the star if you can illustrate each verse.

Characters 1

Here are descriptions of two characters.

Kevin

Kevin likes to tell lots of jokes. He always makes everyone laugh, even our teacher, Miss Taylor. He pulls funny faces and says things in a funny voice. He shares his things with everyone in our class and will always help to look after someone if they are hurt.

Ann

Ann is the class bully. She is always shouting at people to "Go away!" Sometimes she hits people and she calls out a lot in class.
Miss Taylor often tells her off for not sharing things. She never wants to help people if they are hurt.

Write out the words that describe each character in the box below.

Kevin	Ann

Word box

mean   friendly   unkind

nice   nasty   helpful

unhelpful

Write down two more words of your own to describe each character.

Kevin _____

Ann _____

Characters 2

Here are descriptions of two different teachers.

Mrs Day

She gets angry a lot of the time. She shouts at people if they are not listening to her. She bangs her hand on the desk and tells all of her class to stop talking and look at the board.

Mr Ivy

He is very kind and never shouts. If he wants someone to do something he asks them in a quiet voice. If someone is being silly, he waits for them to stop and then carries on with the lesson.

This is **Freddie**, the naughtiest child in Mrs Day's class. What do you think he is saying?

Write inside each speech bubble two things that each teacher might say.

Beginnings and endings

Look at the sentences below. Some are beginnings to stories and some are endings of stories. **Write out each one, putting them into the correct light bulb.**

One day last summer

They all lived happily ever after

Once upon a time

A long, long time ago

And that was the end of that

In a castle on top of a lonely hill

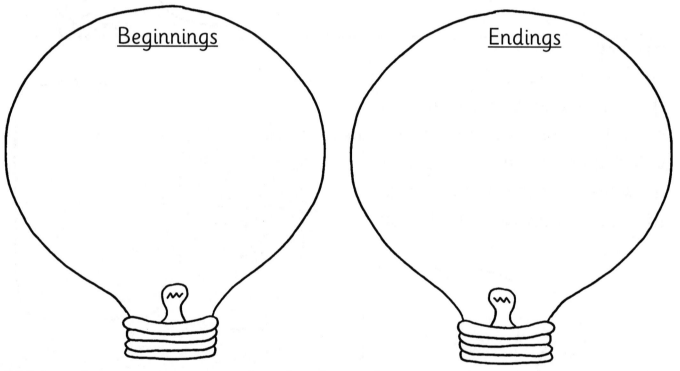

Beginnings

Endings

Write down two more beginnings for a story.

_____   _____

Write down two more endings for a story.

_____   _____

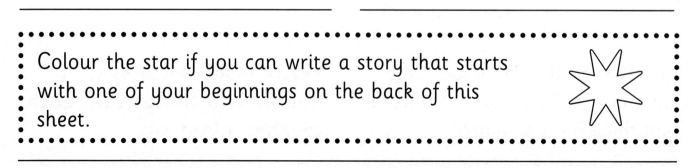

Colour the star if you can write a story that starts with one of your beginnings on the back of this sheet.

Park jumbled sentences

Write the words from each sentence in the right order.

swings are the All red

_____

slide five has steps The

_____

rubbish bin Put your the in

_____

basketball are hoops There two

_____

Write two jumbled sentences of your own. Try them on a friend.

_____   _____

_____

_____

Colour the star if
you can draw some
pictures of your local
park.

Fact or fiction? 1

A fact is something that is true. Fiction is something that is made up.
Write 'fact' or 'fiction' next to each of these sentences.

Pigs can fly._____

Teachers have two heads._____

Grass is green._____

Football is a game. _____

Cats are bigger than lions. _____

Clocks tell you the time. _____

Pizza is a type of animal. _____

Jelly is a type of food. _____

Write down three facts you know.

1. _____

2. _____

3. _____

Make up three pieces of fiction.

1._____

_____

2._____

_____

3._____

_____

Colour the star when
you have read
your pieces of fact
or fiction to a friend.

Fact or fiction? 2

Highlight the 'fact' sentences with a yellow pen and the 'fiction' sentences with a green pen.

The school day starts at five minutes to nine at Homewood Primary School. The headteacher, Mrs Jones, begins her day by flying around the playground on a broomstick. The teachers take their registers and then the first lesson begins. The first lesson each day is about how to ski off the roof of the school. The second lesson is Maths and all of the class do adding up and taking away.

At break time the children play lots of different games. One of the games involves Mrs Jones wearing a purple costume and dancing to very loud music.

In the afternoon, the children sleep for two hours whilst the teachers read comics. The school day finishes at three o'clock. The teachers then go home and the children stay for three hours to tidy up the school.

Write down two facts about your day in school.

_____

_____

Make up a funny piece of fiction about your school day.

_____

_____

Titles 1

Look at the book titles inside the fish. Each one is a title for a book about a sea adventure.

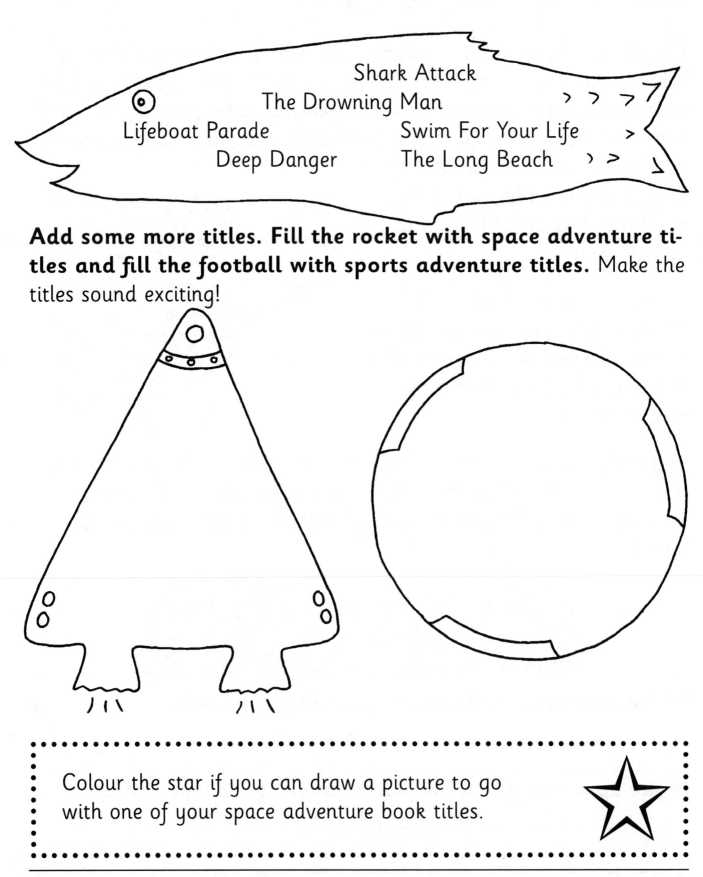

Shark Attack

The Drowning Man

Lifeboat Parade   Swim For Your Life

Deep Danger   The Long Beach

Add some more titles. Fill the rocket with space adventure titles and fill the football with sports adventure titles. Make the titles sound exciting!

Colour the star if you can draw a picture to go with one of your space adventure book titles.

Titles 2

Here are some book titles.

The Horrible Headteacher

The Monkeys Go Wild

A Day on the Moon

The Last Tennis Match

The Chase

The Clown's Party

Match each book title to the book theme.

Book theme	Book title
The circus	
Sport	
Animals	
Space	
School	
Driving	

Make up and write down two new titles for books about animals.

1. _____

2. _____

Colour the star if you can write three sentences about your favourite animal.

Blurbs

The blurb is the piece of writing on the back of a book that tells you what the book is about. Here is a blurb to look at.

Space Battle

On their way home from school, Kim and Clinton are captured by Aliens and taken to the planet Rax in a giant space rocket. Find out how they get home in this funny, fast moving adventure story.

Imagine that Kate and Clinton need to fight the aliens or get taken to another planet by mistake. **Write out your own exciting blurb for this book. Draw a picture.**

_____

_____

_____

_____

_____

_____

Capital letters

The headteacher of Grange Primary School has written a letter to parents. It's about the new school uniform, but she's missed out all the full stops, commas and capital letters. **Help her out by putting in all of the capitals, commas and full stops.**

grange primary school
6 grange road
home town
hn6 2db

2nd september

dear parents
i am writing to you to tell you all about our new school uniform the shirts are green and the trousers and skirts are grey john gregg and tanya bell from year 1 designed the school logo the uniform will be available to buy on monday wednesday and thursday after school from mrs henman in the office i look forward to seeing the children in their new uniforms
yours sincerely

mrs a royal

We need a new school uniform!

Colour the star if you can design a brand new uniform for your school.

Poems on the same theme

Look at these three poems on the theme of 'my sister'.

My sister's silly
  My sister's tall
    My sister climbs
      To the top of the wall
        My sister leaves
          All her clothes in a heap
            My sister's best
              When she's fallen asleep

My sister always says 'Shush!'
When I play games, it's 'Shush!'
When I eat, it's 'Shush!'
When I talk, it's 'Shush!'
When I fight, it's 'Shush!'
When I watch TV, it's 'Shush!'
In fact the only time she doesn't
say 'Shush!'
Is when she's talking

My sister
  What can I say about her?
My sister
  What should I say about her?
My sister
  What will I say about her?
My sister
  I'd better say nothing at all.

Which one of these 'My sister' poems do you like the best and why?

Colour the star if you can illustrate your favourite poem.

© Jonny Zucker

Rhyme time

Read this rhyming poem.

Robbie Gold was on his way.
He knew it was a perfect day
For playing football in the park.
He'd stay outside 'til it was dark.
His mum said, "Keep your trainers clean,
The mud clogs up our washing machine."
But Robbie played with all his might
And soon his trainers were a sight.
For if you looked them up and down
The mud had coloured them all brown.
His mum was waiting at the door,
Said, "What you looking guilty for?"
He tried to hide them from her stare
But she just said, "Now get in there."
The trainers Robbie's mum could see –
He went to bed without his tea.

Find three new rhyming words for each of the words below.

way	clean	door	see
_____	_____	_____	_____
_____	_____	_____	_____
_____	_____	_____	_____

Now have a go at writing your own rhyming poem about going to the park. You can use any of the rhyming words from above if you like.

Colour the star if you can draw a picture of Robbie Gold's mother telling him off about his muddy trainers.

Questions 1

Use the words below to complete the questions.

When ...   What ...   Where ...   Why ...   Which ...   Who ...

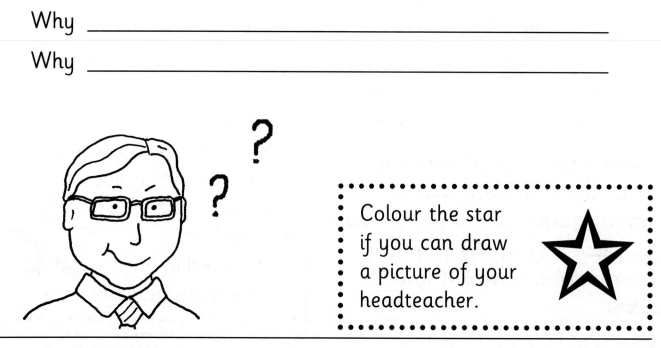

_____ are my trainers?

_____ one of you is playing in goal?

_____ is the captain of the tennis team?

_____ are you looking so sad today?

_____ is it time for us to go home?

_____ are you doing, standing on a chair?

Write down two 'Why' questions you would like to ask the headteacher of your school. Don't forget the question mark at the end of each one.

Why _____

Why _____

Colour the star
if you can draw
a picture of your
headteacher.

Questions 2

Read this passage about a funny king. Using the question words below make up six questions that you'd like to ask him. Don't forget to put a question mark at the end of each question.

The king got up very early one morning and ate twenty pieces of toast for breakfast. After eating he played leapfrog with some frogs he found by the palace pond. Then he slept for two hours and snored very loudly. For lunch he dunked his chips into his ice-cream. After lunch he played a game of football with the palace dogs. By eight o'clock he was very tired so he found a quiet cupboard, climbed inside and went to sleep.

When _____

What _____

Where _____

Why _____

Who _____

Which _____

Dictionaries 1

Use a dictionary to find six words that have something to do with school, for example: classroom, teacher.

Make a list and then write them out in alphabetical order.

_____   1. _____

_____   2. _____

_____   3. _____

_____   4. _____

_____   5. _____

_____   6. _____

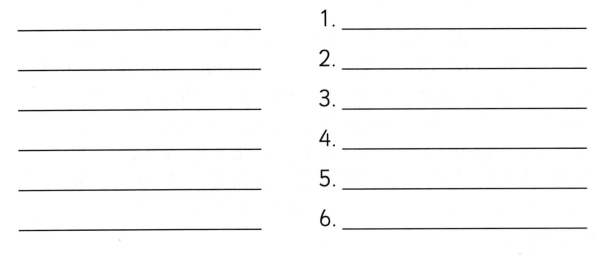

Write three sentences using three of the words you have found.

_____

_____

_____

Colour the star
if you can draw
a picture of your
classroom.

Dictionaries 2

A 'definition' is the writing beside the word in a dictionary. It explains what the word means.

Find these words in a dictionary and write out the dictionary 'definition' for each one.

house _____

hand _____

hear _____

hot _____

Without using a dictionary, write definitions for these words.

snow _____

sun _____

shout _____

sit _____

Jack is trying to think of 10 words beginning with 'sh'. Use your dictionary to help him.

Favourite food alphabet list

Write a list of your eight favourite foods. Use a dictionary to check your spelling.

1. _____   5. _____

2. _____   6. _____

3. _____   7. _____

4. _____   8. _____

Now re-write the list, but put it in alphabetical order.

1. _____   5. _____

2. _____   6. _____

3. _____   7. _____

4. _____   8. _____

Write a silly sentence that has three of the foods in it.

_____

_____

_____

_____

_____

Colour the star if you can draw a picture to go with your sentence.

Class register

Here are some names from a class register.
Write out the names again putting them in alphabetical order.

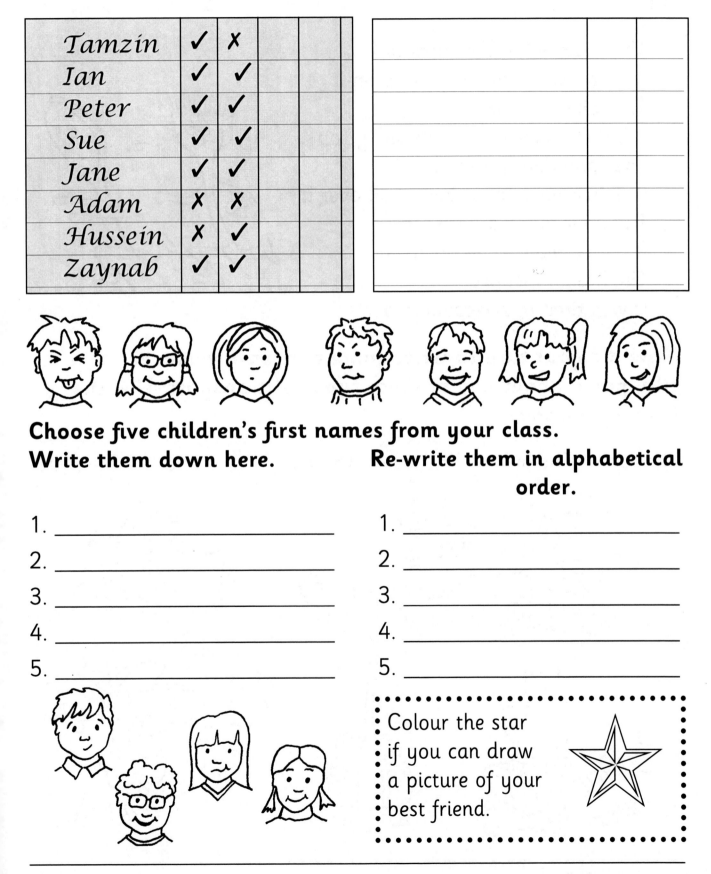

Tamzin	✓	✗			
Ian	✓	✓			
Peter	✓	✓			
Sue	✓	✓			
Jane	✓	✓			
Adam	✗	✗			
Hussein	✗	✓			
Zaynab	✓	✓			

Choose five children's first names from your class. Write them down here.

Re-write them in alphabetical order.

1. _____

2. _____

3. _____

4. _____

5. _____

1. _____

2. _____

3. _____

4. _____

5. _____

Colour the star
if you can draw
a picture of your
best friend.

What a load of rubbish!

Some poems don't make any sense at all. They can be silly and very funny. Poems like these are called **nonsense poems**. Look at this one.

The chair hid in the cupboard
It didn't want anyone sitting on it
The table ran away
It didn't want mess on its shiny top
The spoon disappeared
It didn't want soup slurped all over it
The door made a dash for it
It didn't want to be slammed
The broom escaped
It was tired of sweeping floors.

Now it's your turn to write some nonsense verse. Write a silly poem about one of these types of transport. Use the back of the sheet.

The car   The bus   The train   The bike   The boat   The plane

Question marks

A question always has a question mark at the end.

Decide which of these phrases needs a question mark and which needs an exclamation mark. Put in the correct mark.

Why are you so late for school

Stop that now

Not now, I'm busy

Which is the best way to the park

Where is my computer game

Go away from me

Hurry up or we'll be late

How did you know I was here

Write down one question for each person.

Key words 1

The key words in a passage are the words that are the most important or tell us the most interesting things about a subject.

Underline the key words in this passage about card tricks.

Card tricks look really great if they are done well, but it takes a lot of practice to get them right. One of the most famous tricks is called the 'Rising cards', where the magician seems to make some cards float in the air. If you become a very clever magician you can show your tricks to people in theatres and ask them to pay money to see you. The very best magicians have their own shows on television and earn lots of money by performing their magic tricks.

Make up a sentence of your own using one of the key words.

_____

_____

_____

_____

. . . .

Colour the star if you can write two sentences about what it must be like to be a magician.

. . . .

Key words 2

Look at the passage below. It is all about making a music CD. Underline the key words.

To make a CD, a pop group needs to practise a song until it sounds good. Then they go to a place called a studio and sing their song. It is recorded onto a special computer. The computer puts the song onto a CD. This is called the 'master'. Thousands of other CDs are copied from the master. An artist does a picture or takes a photo for the cover of the CD. The finished CDs are put into cases and go to the shops. Then we get a chance to buy them.

Write out the key words here.

_____

_____

_____

Make up a sentence of your own using one of the key words.

_____

_____

_____

Colour the star if you can write two sentences about your favourite pop group or favourite song.

Cartoon strip 1

Look at the four pictures in this cartoon strip. The pictures tell a story but there are no words. **Write what is happening on the lines below the pictures.**

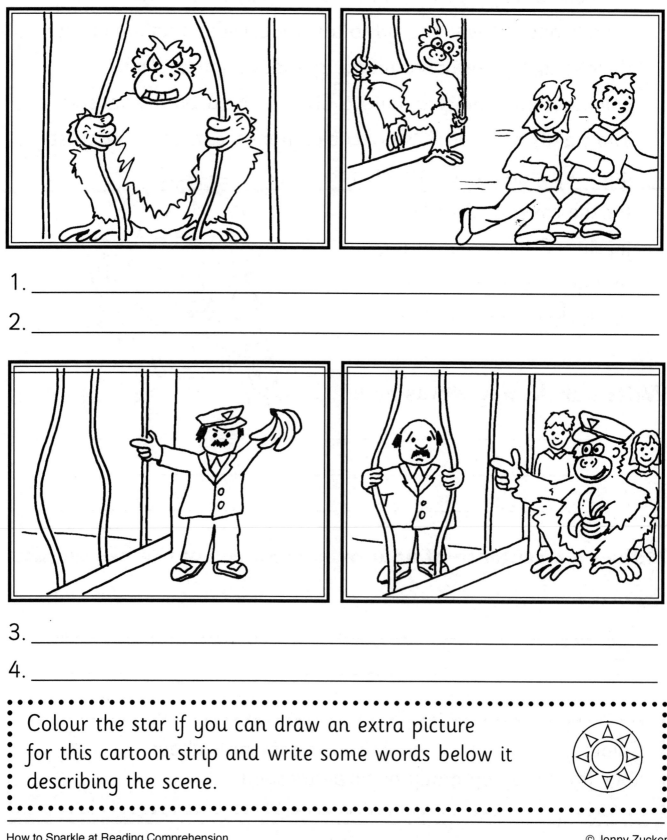

1. _____

2. _____

3. _____

4. _____

Colour the star if you can draw an extra picture for this cartoon strip and write some words below it describing the scene.

Cartoon strip 2

Look at the four pictures in this cartoon strip. The pictures tell a story but there are no words. **Write what is happening on the lines below the pictures.**

1. _____

2. _____

3. _____

4. _____

Colour the star if you can write what the teacher might have said to the girl when he was telling her off.

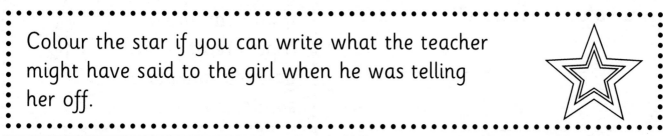

Passports please!

Look at this passport. It belongs to a teacher called Miss Small.

Name: Miss Small
Age: 27
Eye colour: Brown
Hair colour: Blonde
Country of birth: England
Favourite colour: Blue
Favourite food: Fish and chips
Country you most want to visit: India

Write in the details for your own passport. Draw a picture of yourself in the photo space.

Name:
Age:
Eye colour:
Hair colour:
Country of birth:
Favourite colour:
Favourite food:
Country you most want to visit:

If you could go on holiday today, which friends would you take with you?

1. _____

2. _____

Colour the star if you can draw a picture of yourself making a sandcastle.

Posters

Look at this poster for a football match.

Fenton Park play Hove United
A great day out for all the family.
The winning team win a shiny gold cup.
DON'T MISS IT.

Date: This Saturday
Time: 3 o'clock
Cost: Adults £5, Children £2
Place: Fenton Park

Imagine that a circus is coming to town. Create your own poster for the circus. Remember to include the date, the time, the cost, the place and a name for the circus.

Colour the star if you can decorate your poster.

It's play time!

Read this story and fill in the missing words from the box below.

It was _____ o'clock and time for play. Dave and Kate

_____ into the playground.

"Let's play_____" shouted

Kate.

"OK." replied Dave "We can use

our _____ for goals."

Lots of other _____

joined in with the game, but Kate

was the _____.

"When I'm older," Kate said, "I

want to be captain of the school

football _____."

Just then, the _____ rang and

the football match had to stop.

| team | ran | children | ten |
| best | football | jumpers | bell |

Now write three sentences about your school play time.

_____

_____

_____

TV choice

Read this story and fill in the missing words from the box below.

Dean is _____ years old and loves watching _____. As soon as he gets _____ from school he _____ it on. His favourite _____ is Football Stars and is all _____ the world's best football _____. Dean's mum is always _____, "Dean, you watch far too _____ telly. Haven't you got any homework to do?"

Dean doesn't really listen to her. He is far too busy _____ the TV!

```
home        saying      programme      players       watching

about       six         television     switches      much
```

Colour the star if you can write the names of your favourite TV programmes.

The farm trip

Read this short story and answer the questions on the next page.

Mr Wood's class were going on a school trip to a farm. The coach arrived outside the school gates at nine o'clock. "Come along," called Mr Wood to all the children. "If we don't get a move on we will be very late."

The coach trip took forty minutes and everyone was very excited when they stopped outside the front of the farm. The farmer was waiting for them with his sheepdog. First of all he took the class to the cowsheds. It was milking time and everyone watched as the machines collected all of the cow's milk.

Next he took them to the sheep pen and to see the pigs. The pig sties were very smelly and Mr Wood told everyone to hold their noses! After that they visited the chicken coop and saw three hens fighting each other.

Mr Wood then said it was time for the picnic lunch. Everyone had brought a packed lunch and the class sat in a quiet field eating and drinking. At the end of lunch, the farmer came round with a black bin bag to collect all the rubbish.

"Right," said the farmer, "there's one more thing to see and it's very special." Everyone followed him to a barn and the farmer told the class to keep very quiet. Inside the barn was a horse with a tiny foal. The foal was only two days old and was tiny.

It was time to go home. The class got back on the coach and waved to the farmer and his sheepdog. "What a great day!" smiled Mr Wood "You've all been fantastic!"

The farmer waved back as the coach pulled away and his sheepdog barked.

The farm trip, questions

1. Where were Mr Wood's class going?

   _____

2. What time did the coach arrive?

   _____

3. Why did Mr Wood call to the children?

   _____

4. How long did the coach journey take?

   _____

5. What were the first three places the farmer showed them?

   _____

6. What was happening in the chicken coop?

   _____

7. How did the farmer help clear up after lunch?

   _____

8. What was the 'special' thing the farmer showed them?

   _____

9. Why do you think the farmer asked everyone to be quiet when
   they were looking at the horse and foal?

   _____

10. How did the farmer and his sheepdog say goodbye to the class?

    _____

Playground problems

Read this short story and answer the questions on the next page.

At Deepdale Primary School the Year 1 and Year 2 children were always fighting over who could use the Red Court to play football.

"It's our turn," said the Year 1 children.

"It's our turn," said the Year 2 children.

Mr Rice, the headteacher, walked into the playground and called,

"I've had enough of this, stop it right now!"

All of the children stopped arguing and listened to him.

"I've decided," said Mr Rice, "that things are not working out in this playground and so I have written a Red Court timetable."

He walked over to the wall and pinned up a white piece of paper.

It said Monday – Year 1, Tuesday - Year 2, Wednesday – Year 1, Thursday – Year 2, Friday – Reception class.

Most of the children nodded and said they thought that was a good idea.

"The timetable is to begin straight away," said Mr Rice, and since it was a Tuesday it was Year 2's turn. For the rest of the week the timetable worked out very well and the fighting over the Red Court stopped.

By Friday, Mr Rice was really pleased with the way things had worked out. He took a special assembly to say 'Well done' to the Year 1 and Year 2 children for sticking to the Red Court timetable.

"Sometimes timetables are a good idea," he told them, smiling.

Monday – Year 1
Tuesday – Year 2
Wednesday – Year 1

Thursday – Year 2
Friday –
Reception class

Playground problems, questions

1. What was the name of the school in the story?

   _____

2. What were the Year 1 and Year 2 children fighting about?

   _____

3. Why do you think Mr Rice shouted out in the playground?

   _____

4. Why did the children stop arguing?

   _____

5. How had Mr Rice decided to stop all the fighting?

   _____

6. On which days were Year 1 going to get the Red Court?

   _____

7. What did most of the children think about Mr Rice's plan?

   _____

8. Whose turn was it to use the Red Court that day?

   _____

9. Did the timetable work?

   _____

10. How did Mr Rice feel at the end of the week?

   _____

School play

Read this short story and answer the questions on the next page.

It was seven o'clock and the school play was about to begin. Seven-year-old Sam was playing the part of Jack in 'Jack and the Beanstalk'. He was very excited but felt a bit funny in his tummy.

"Don't worry," said Miss Day, his teacher, "you are going to be great."

Suddenly the curtains opened and then the music started to play.

Miss Day nodded at Sam and he ran onto the stage and shouted "Good evening, everybody!"

Everybody in the audience shouted, "Good evening," back at him. Then Annie walked onto the stage. She was playing the part of his mother.

Sam and Annie began to act out the story of Jack and the Beanstalk and before long Sam was climbing the beanstalk. This was a long ladder covered in paper leaves of all colours. There were lots of other children in the play, but Sam and Annie had the main parts.

At the end of the show the audience clapped and cheered for two minutes. They loved it!

Sam and Annie took a bow and ran off stage. Miss Day was also clapping herself. She was so pleased. "You both did very well" she said, smiling at them.

"I really enjoyed that," said Annie.

"So did I," replied Sam, "but I'm glad it's all over!"

School play, questions

1. How old was Sam? _____

2. What was the name of the school play? _____

   _____

3. Why did Sam have a funny feeling in his tummy? _____

   _____

4. What did Miss Day say to Sam? _____

   _____

5. What happened after the curtains opened? _____

   _____

6. Where did Sam go after Miss Day nodded at him? _____

   _____

7. What part was Annie playing? _____

8. What was the beanstalk made out of? _____

   _____

9. Why did the audience clap and cheer at the end of the show?

   _____

10. How did Sam feel at the end of the play? _____

   _____

Extension ideas

Classroom labels – page 6. Ask the children to draw a picture of their bedroom at home and label as many items in it as they can.

Rollerblade instructions – page 8. Ask the children to think of the main dangers involved in rollerblading. Make a class list of these and discuss safety measures that can be used when rollerblading.

Class lesson chart – page 9. Draw the weekly class timetable on the board. Ask the children to copy out the timetable and to give a rating 1–10 of how much they enjoy each lesson.

Characters 1 and 2 – pages 14 and 15. Choose two famous fairy tale characters, such as The Big Bad Wolf from Red Riding Hood, and Snow White. Get groups of children to draw large pictures of these characters. Display the pictures and below them place a large blank piece of paper. Whenever a child can think of a characteristic belonging to either character, they can write it up on this sheet.

Fact or fiction? 1 and 2 – pages 18 and 19. Using information books, get the children to write out some facts and make up some fiction about a particular topic of interest to them.

Poems on the same theme – page 24. Ask the children to write poems about their brothers, parents or other family members.

Questions 2 – page 27. Write a full adventure story about the funny king. Describe more of his activities and create a queen character and perhaps some little princes and princesses.

Favourite food alphabet list – page 30. As a class, design a menu for your favourite foods. Think of a name for a new café or restaurant. Use the class computer to design and print out the finished menu.

Class register – page 31. Give each child a complete list of the names in your class in non-alphabetical order. Can they write out all the children's names beginning with the letter … ?

Question marks – page 33. Draw a question mark and an exclamation mark on two separate sheets of paper. Either ask the children a question or say an exclamation, and get them to decide as a class which it is.

Cartoon strip 1 and 2 – pages 36 and 37. Cut out cartoon strips from comics. Get the children to paste a sequence of pictures into their book/onto paper, writing their own scripts/captions underneath.

Playground problems – page 44. Discuss as a class what the main playground problems are in your school. Make a list of them and try to come up with possible solutions.

Lightning Source UK Ltd.
Milton Keynes UK
UKOW01f1010220813

215729UK00001B/20/P